REBEL GIRLS AWESOME ENTREPRENEURS

25 TALES OF WOMEN BUILDING BUSINESSES

Good Night Stories for Rebel Girls and Rebel Girls are registered trademarks.
Good Night Stories for Rebel Girls and all other Rebel Girls titles are available for bulk purchase for sale promotions, premiums, fundraising, and educational needs.
For details, write to sales@rebelgirls.com.

This is a work of creative nonfiction. It is a collection of heartwarming and thought-provoking stories inspired by the lives and adventures of 25 influential women. It is not an encyclopedic account of the events and accomplishments of their lives.

www.rebelgirls.com

Some of the artwork in this book has been previously published in the books *Good Night Stories for Rebel Girls 2* and *Good Night Stories for Rebel Girls: 100 Immigrant Women Who Changed the World*.

Choosing only 25 women to spotlight in this book was difficult. Special thanks to the following individuals who helped us nominate an incredible cadre of women to feature: Adeyemi Ajao, Ann Miura-Ko, April Underwood, Cack Wilhelm, Christina Miller, Fern Mandelbaum, Jocelyn Mangan, Julia Boorstin Samuelson, Laura Melahn, Mar Hershenson, Nicole Johnson, Tatyana Mamut, Vanessa Larco

Text by Abby Sher, Sarah Parvis, Nana Brew-Hammond, Carla Sinclair, and Susanna Daniel
Art direction by Giulia Flamini
Cover illustrations by Annalisa Ventura
Graphic design by Annalisa Ventura and Kristen Brittain
Special thanks: Grace House, Jes Wolfe, Maithy Vu, Marina Asenjo, Vivian Mangan

Printed in Canada, 2022
10 9 8 7 6 5 4 3 2 1
ISBN: 978-1-953424-23-5

CONTENTS

FOREWORD

Hi Rebels,

Growing up, I was constantly making things. I would make handbags out of takeout containers and process black-and-white photos in my middle school darkroom. I didn't know at the time that I would start my own business encouraging other kids to make things too—everything from cardboard catapults and felt capes to wooden clocks and arcade games. But I did—and it's been a lot of fun. It's also been a lot of creative hard work.

Have you ever thought about starting your own business? If you are reading this book, there's a good chance you have. And that's really exciting! The world can always use more curious, energetic people who spot a problem and then create a product or a service to solve it. That's how I got started.

When my kids were young, I wanted them to have lots of hands-on experiences making, building, and tinkering with things—like I did when I was little. I couldn't find what I wanted in the market, so I made it myself. And that's how my company, KiwiCo, was born. Now, we've sent out more than 25 million crates filled with all the materials and inspiration kids need to experiment, create, and explore.

As you'll see in these stories, successful entrepreneurs often build businesses around their own interests.

What do you love to do? What problem do you want to solve?

Mikaila Ulmer's entrepreneurial journey started when she was four years old. After being stung by a bee, she learned all about them. Then she turned her love for bees into a business making honey-sweetened lemonade. Kathy Hannun turned her desire to protect the planet into a business using natural heat from under the Earth's surface to heat and cool homes.

Solveiga Pakštaitė found out that tons of safe, healthy food is thrown away every year because of the sell-by dates that are printed on packaging. She knows food waste is a huge problem. So she got to work inventing a special kind of label that would change from smooth to bumpy to let people—including visually impaired people—know when food has expired.

The women in this book have started more than 30 businesses. The companies they have founded, built, or run employ more than 50,000 people today. And the investors in these pages have invested millions of dollars to support the visions of creative, hard-working entrepreneurs. They've had an enormous impact.

All of the women in this book have also gone through the ups and downs of entrepreneurship. If their experiences were anything like mine, I'm sure they learned a lot along the way. I am inspired and energized by their stories, and I hope you are too.

Read on to learn more about how 25 incredible entrepreneurs and executives brought their business ideas to life, find out about the importance of investors, and do activities that will help you dream up a business of your own.

Entrepreneurship is a roller coaster. Welcome aboard!

—Sandra Oh Lin, Founder and CEO, KiwiCo

SCAN TO HEAR MORE!

BONUS! AUDIO STORIES!

Download the Rebel Girls app to hear longer stories about some of the impactful business leaders in this book. You will also unlock creative activities and discover stories of other trailblazing women. Whenever you come across a bookmark icon, scan the code, and you'll be whisked away on an audio adventure.

AILEEN LEE

FOUNDER AND INVESTOR

Once there was a girl who dreamed of unicorns. But her unicorns weren't mythical creatures. They were incredible businesses.

In 1970, in New York, an immigrant couple from China had a baby named Aileen. Throughout her girlhood, Aileen heard stories of how hard her family had worked and how many jobs they'd held. She listened and understood how important it was to respect their achievements.

By the time she was in high school, Aileen had started several businesses of her own. With friends, she made and sold tie-dye T-shirts, with bright yellow sunbursts and splashes of blue and green. They even tried selling egg rolls at busy nearby street fairs. "My parents probably spent more money on the gas driving me to different jobs than I made," she said.

Aileen wasn't afraid of hard work. And she had a knack for knowing which businesses would succeed and why. She's now the founder and managing partner of Cowboy Ventures, a firm that invests money in entrepreneurs to build new businesses. It's one of the first female-led venture capital firms in the world.

To girls who are interested in starting companies, Aileen suggests investigating problems that you have a personal connection to, then finding a solution. But the solution can't just be a little bit better—it has to be a lot better than anything that already exists.

Aileen knows the hard truth. Most businesses fail. To succeed, she says, a founder must be willing to work through the highs and lows.

She coined the term *unicorn* to refer to companies valued at $1 billion or more. They're rare, but with investors like her, there are sure to be more soon.

BORN MARCH 17, 1970

UNITED STATES OF AMERICA

ILLUSTRATION BY
KATHRIN HONESTA

"WHEN I WAS GROWING
UP, I WAS NOT TAUGHT TO
TALK ABOUT MONEY OR
TO TALK ABOUT MAKING
MONEY, OR TO THINK THAT
TRYING TO MAKE MONEY
WAS COOL.... THAT'S
SUPER WRONG."
—AILEEN LEE

ANJALI SUD

BUSINESS EXECUTIVE

When Anjali was a young girl, she dreamed of becoming a playwright. In her basement, she sang and danced and created scenarios for her siblings to act out. But as she grew older, Anjali realized that her real passion was business. So when she was about to graduate from college, Anjali set her sights on banking. She applied to dozens of powerful companies. To her disappointment, none of them would hire her. Many said she just "wasn't the right fit." She felt rejected but didn't give up. Instead, Anjali refocused her job search. She applied to smaller companies, and eventually, went to work for an online video platform called Vimeo.

That's when she faced another greater challenge. Vimeo was struggling to compete with larger video platforms. These companies had millions and millions of subscribers who were posting videos on their sites. No matter what Vimeo tried, it couldn't grow an audience to match its larger rivals. And without a bigger audience, it might fail. How could Anjali battle such giants to make her company more popular?

And then, like a lightning bolt striking Earth, an idea hit her! Instead of battling the bigwigs by competing, why not make Vimeo different from them? Anjali reinvented the company by offering creators and businesses online tools to help them make videos look amazing. Vimeo would also allow their customers to distribute their videos to other social media sites, turning their competitors into partners. After proving this idea worked, Anjali was promoted to chief executive officer (CEO).

As CEO, Anjali has grown Vimeo into a billion-dollar company. With creativity and fresh thinking, she's writing her own story.

BORN AUGUST 13, 1983
UNITED STATES OF AMERICA

"LOOK WHERE OTHERS
AREN'T LOOKING."
—ANJALI SUD

ANN MIURA-KO

FOUNDER AND INVESTOR

"**P**lease, please, please," Ann begged. She was just two years old, and she knew that, more than anything, she wanted to take violin lessons. Ann was different than the rest of the kids she knew. In third grade, she explored her native language by creating Japanese letters for her computer. And in fifth grade, she signed up for an adult business class.

In her twenties, Ann couldn't figure out what she wanted to be. A farmer? A doctor? A lawyer? Nothing sounded quite right—that is, until she took a simple job filing papers at Yale University and met an important CEO. This CEO invited her to shadow—or follow—him around his workplace at a giant technology company. Ann said yes!

Afterwards, the CEO sent her two photos in the mail. One was of her sitting in a huge white chair facing him, and the other was of the famous software developer and philanthropist Bill Gates sitting in the exact same chair facing the same CEO. Suddenly, everything seemed possible. *Why can't I run a big company too?* Ann thought.

It was rare to see a woman or an Asian American at the head of a venture capital firm, but Ann didn't let that slow her down. She did her research, cofounded her own venture capital company called Floodgate, invested in many new businesses, and became known as "the most powerful woman in startups."

While male venture capitalists usually invested money in technology firms, Ann took chances on businesses they often ignored, like clothing companies. She couldn't be exactly like all the men around her, so she decided to do what she did best: be different. And it worked!

BORN NOVEMBER 27, 1976

UNITED STATES OF AMERICA

"DIFFERENCES CAN
ACTUALLY BE AN
IMPORTANT PART OF WHO
YOU ARE, CAN HELP YOU
STAND OUT, CAN HELP YOU
BE MEMORABLE."
—ANN MIURA-KO

ASMA ISHAQ

ENTREPRENEUR AND BUSINESS EXECUTIVE

Once upon a time, there was a girl named Asma who had a lot to say but was very shy. Kids at school teased her and called her "asthma," but instead of correcting them, Asma walked away or disappeared into a book. Books were Asma's best friends. She loved how a single idea could take her on a trip around the world. Asma knew she had great ideas too. She just had to believe in herself.

Asma's father worked at a company that made vitamins. One day, Asma watched as he and his team studied different minerals that could help people get stronger and healthier. She decided she wanted to do that too.

So Asma studied hard in school and became the first woman in her family to go to college. Once she got there, she took every science class she could find, like biology, chemistry, and psychology. She spent hours in a lab, extracting DNA from different cells. DNA is the code that tells the body how to grow and function. Asma was determined to find new ways to encourage people to live healthfully.

And she did! In 2008, Asma started her own health and wellness company. It made natural products and gave vitamins to underserved families. It was scary for Asma, putting her heart and soul into this one idea and being the voice of her brand. But in the past 14 years, Asma has transformed her idea into Modere, the fastest growing company led by a woman in the whole world!

Asma believes the only way she feels strong is when she helps others feel strong. And she's not too shy to say that out loud.

BORN OCTOBER 28, 1975
UNITED STATES OF AMERICA

ILLUSTRATION BY
XUAN LOC XUAN

"GIRLS CAN DO
ANYTHING."
—ASMA ISHAQ

JENNIFER DOUDNA

BIOCHEMIST AND ENTREPRENEUR

Not long ago, Jennifer was startled out of bed by her phone. "Hello?" she said, rubbing her eyes.

A reporter asked what she thought about the Nobel Prize. The Nobel Prize is the most prestigious award a scientist can earn! "Whose Nobel Prize?" she asked.

"You don't know?" the reporter squealed. "You won the Nobel Prize in Chemistry!"

Jennifer, who grew up playing in the enchanting rain forests of Hawaii, is the scientist who co-invented CRISPR. Some people call this amazing tool "molecular scissors." These tiny scissors can be used inside a person's body to cut or edit genes that cause diseases like cancer.

News about Jennifer's invention spread like wildfire, and labs all around the planet wanted it. But CRISPR wasn't ready for the world quite yet.

Jennifer had questions. *What are all the diseases CRISPR can snip (even before they make someone sick)? Are there other good reasons to edit genes? Are there dangers?* To find the answers, she would need help from a huge team of scientists. She'd also need to build countless new tools.

Even though she was world-famous as a scientist, Jennifer also became a businesswoman. She cofounded not one but five different companies to solve CRISPR's wonderful mysteries and explore its exciting capabilities. And while she continues her research, CRISPR is already beginning to save lives.

Not only did Jennifer's love of science steer her to become a powerful business leader, but her stunning invention has also changed the future of medicine.

BORN FEBRUARY 19, 1964

UNITED STATES OF AMERICA

"GROWING UP, I WAS TOLD MORE THAN A FEW TIMES THAT GIRLS DON'T DO CHEMISTRY, OR GIRLS DON'T DO SCIENCE—FORTUNATELY I IGNORED THAT!"
—JENNIFER DOUDNA

ILLUSTRATION BY
IRENE RINALDI

JULIE CHEN

ENVIRONMENTALIST AND ENTREPRENEUR

In China, where Julie was born, forests full of tall, magical plants stretch as far as the eye can see. These plants have woody stems and grow super fast—three feet per day! They grow well without chemical pesticides or fertilizer or even much water. They also absorb 35% more carbon and produce 30% more oxygen than trees.

These incredible plants are called bamboo.

As an adult, Julie lived in London. But when she was in China visiting her parents, she got a career-changing idea. During the long drive from the airport, she gazed out the window at miles and miles of bamboo forests.

She knew that 27,000 trees were cut down every day to make something everyone uses: toilet paper! *What if*, Julie thought, *we made toilet paper and tissues out of bamboo instead? Think of all the forests, wildlife, and water we'd save.*

She already knew a lot about marketing because she was running a shoe business. Her new venture could use her skills—and it would reflect her values.

Julie launched her eco-friendly paper company in 2016. She called it the Cheeky Panda because people associate pandas with bamboo and because *cheeky* means "fun" in England. When her friends pointed out that cheeky might also refer to one's posterior—or butt!—Julie laughed. "I thought 'cheeky' was just 'fun,'" she said.

In 2020, when COVID-19 hit and people were forced to stay home, stores all over the world ran out of toilet paper. The big toilet paper manufacturers couldn't keep up with demand, and the Cheeky Panda's sales quadrupled. Julie was happy to help households while saving trees too!

BORN JULY 4, 1981
CHINA AND UNITED KINGDOM

"BELIEVE IN YOURSELF,
AND OTHERS WILL
BELIEVE IN YOU."
—JULIE CHEN

KATHY HANNUN

ENGINEER AND ENTREPRENEUR

Thousands of butterflies fluttered into the gardens of Durham, New Hampshire, and nobody loved them more than young Kathy. Every fall, she captured caterpillars, feeding them milkweed until they turned into bright orange monarchs. Then she'd set them free.

But in middle school, Kathy had trouble finding caterpillars. Butterflies no longer dotted the sky. Climate change was causing her favorite insects and other wildlife to disappear. She wanted to find ways to bring them back.

After college, Kathy joined a secret team of futuristic inventors who were working to make "impossible" ideas possible. She let herself dream big. She knew using fossil fuels to heat buildings was hurting the planet. So she imagined a new future—a future where geothermal energy (natural heat found under the Earth's surface) would be used instead of oil to heat buildings.

In the beginning, it truly did seem like an "impossible" idea. Starting a business is expensive, and Kathy had to sleep on friends' couches and borrow their cars to save money. She got stuck trying to invent the drills and pipes needed to reach the energy deep underground in an affordable way. She'd never done anything like this before! People shook their heads, saying it couldn't be done. But her drive to fight climate change kept her going.

And she succeeded! Kathy cofounded Dandelion Energy, raised more than $65 million, and grew Dandelion into the largest geothermal heating and cooling company in the United States. As Dandelion's president, she is helping to create a planet-friendly future where people can stay warm in their houses all winter long without damaging the climate.

BORN NOVEMBER 16, 1986
UNITED STATES OF AMERICA

"YOU PRACTICE, YOU PERSIST, YOU GAIN SKILLS, AND YOU BECOME BETTER."
—KATHY HANNUN

ILLUSTRATION BY FABIOLA F. ALDRETE SOLORIO

KATRINA LAKE

ENTREPRENEUR

When Katrina was a kid, she never set up a lemonade stand or held a bake sale. She never thought of herself as an entrepreneur. *That was for people who liked taking risks*, she thought.

But after studying to become a doctor, Katrina's vision of her future changed. She started working for a group of venture capitalists, where she constantly saw people come in and ask investors for money to start their companies. After nearly 100 pitches, Katrina realized these people weren't any more qualified than she was. They were just ordinary folks, like everyone she knew. *Anyone can be an entrepreneur*, she thought. *I could do it too!*

She developed an original business plan where people with great fashion sense would help customers who needed advice or were just too busy to shop. The stylists would put together outfits, pack them in boxes, and mail them out. She named her service Stitch Fix.

Katrina called some friends to help her start Stitch Fix out of her small apartment. Customers immediately signed up. Pretty soon, her business was bursting at the seams. Boxes lined the walls and covered the floors. Katrina desperately needed more money to grow her company.

She found an investor who believed in her and, on Valentine's Day in 2011, he invested $750,000 in her clever idea. Other investors joined in. Stitch Fix moved out of Katrina's small apartment and became a huge company, employing more than 5,800 people.

Katrina eventually took the company public—a huge milestone for any business. At the time, she was the youngest woman to achieve this feat!

BORN DECEMBER 24, 1982

UNITED STATES OF AMERICA

"THE MORE YOU THINK IS
POSSIBLE, THE MORE IS
ACTUALLY POSSIBLE."
—KATRINA LAKE

MADAM C.J. WALKER

INVENTOR AND ENTREPRENEUR

Sarah Breedlove worked long hours, washing clothes in St. Louis, Missouri. It was around 1890, and she earned just $1.50 a day. At night, she took care of her daughter, went to school, and sang in the church choir.

Then she started losing her hair.

Sarah didn't know what was going on. She tried different creams and rinses, but nothing helped. At the time, most beauty products were made for white people, and they didn't work for Sarah. She decided to experiment with different ingredients, and soon, her hair grew back full and healthy.

Before Sarah began marketing her invention, she wanted a unique name as a businesswoman. She found the perfect one and began going door to door selling "Madam C.J. Walker's Wonderful Hair Grower." As Madam, she developed a whole hair care routine known as the Walker System. It combined homemade pomade (scented oils), heated iron combs, and a style of brushing that stimulated hair growth. Black women loved it.

Madam crisscrossed the country giving demonstrations, which were so popular that she had to train other women as "Walker agents" to travel and sell her products too. Customers bought her ointments, shampoos, and conditioners at churches and club meetings, and even by mail order. At one point, her company employed more than 3,000 people—mostly Black women! She also opened a beauty school and factory in Pittsburgh, Pennsylvania, and donated a lot of her earnings to Black education charities.

Madam C.J. Walker became the first self-made female millionaire in the US. More importantly, she helped Black women feel confident and proud.

DECEMBER 23, 1867–MAY 25, 1919

UNITED STATES OF AMERICA

ILLUSTRATION BY
CRISTINA SPANO

"I GOT MY START BY
GIVING MYSELF A START."
—MADAM C.J. WALKER

MAGI RICHANI

ENGINEER AND ENTREPRENEUR

Young Magi was always bringing home stray cats and dogs and then finding them homes. She hated to see animals suffer.

When she was 18, her life changed dramatically. Magi's mother put her and her brother on a plane from their hometown of Beirut, Lebanon, to Austin, Texas. She wanted her children to have more opportunities.

After attending college, Magi went on to graduate school, learning all about civil engineering and project management.

"I love math and science. And I love taking an idea on paper and building on it," she said.

There was something else Magi loved—something she didn't think much about until suddenly she couldn't have it. In her twenties, Magi was diagnosed with lactose intolerance, which meant she could no longer eat one of her favorite foods: cheese!

"Cheese is so delicious and addictive," said Magi. "I could not accept a world where I could never eat it."

Instead of cutting cheese out of her diet, she studied it. Cheese is made by adding enzymes to milk. It causes a protein called casein to clump up. Casein is only produced by mammals that make milk after giving birth. It takes six pounds of feed and an average of 628 gallons of water to produce just ONE gallon of milk! And Magi knew most cows live unhappy lives on factory farms.

"The food system is not good for our animals or our planet," she said.

It took five years, but eventually Magi's company, Nobell Foods, figured out how to make delicious cheeses from all kinds from plants. Not only is Magi's cheese delicious, but it's also much healthier for the planet.

BORN JANUARY 10, 1989

LEBANON AND UNITED STATES OF AMERICA

ILLUSTRATION BY
CARIBAY MB

"FIND A PROBLEM
YOU HAVE AND TRY
TO SOLVE IT."
—MAGI RICHANI

MAR HERSHENSON

FOUNDER AND INVESTOR

O nce there was a girl in Barcelona, Spain, who loved math as much as she loved playing soccer. She found patterns in everything she saw and added up numbers in her head just for fun. In other words, Mar was one smart kid. But she didn't always feel that way.

She didn't have a lot of confidence.

During her first weeks at Stanford University, one of the most prestigious schools in the world, Mar was convinced the college didn't really want her. Whenever she had a question in class, she was too embarrassed to raise her hand. She was worried that she might sound dumb. Finally, when she thought she'd never be able to do the kind of research work her fellow students were doing, she went home and told her boyfriend, "I quit."

But he reminded her that in sports, it's better to "play up"—meaning to play with athletes who are better than you, because it will make you try harder and improve faster. He then asked, *Do you want to be the smartest person, or do you want to learn something?*

These words were like little seeds of confidence that slowly grew inside her. Mar began to ask questions, and she realized it was okay if she made mistakes.

Once her confidence bloomed, Mar cofounded three companies. She became so good at being an entrepreneur that she decided to advise other entrepreneurs. She cofounded Pear Ventures, where she now listens to people pitch smart startup ideas and invests money in those she believes in most—like DoorDash, a company that took off like a rocket! (It has made billions of dollars since she invested in them.) Mar also helps grow companies by giving them advice. And her best advice? Prepare, practice, and have confidence.

BORN JUNE 30, 1971

SPAIN AND UNITED STATES OF AMERICA

ILLUSTRATION BY
MAJU BENGEL

"EVEN WHEN I'D GO OUTSIDE
ON THE PLAYGROUND, I WAS
LOOKING FOR PATTERNS AND
DOING MATH IN MY HEAD, WHICH
DROVE MY PARENTS NUTS."
—MAR HERSHENSON

MARGARETE STEIFF

SEAMSTRESS AND ENTREPRENEUR

When Margarete was just a baby growing up in southern Germany, she got sick with polio. Her legs and right hand were paralyzed. But that didn't stop Margarete from going on lots of adventures with her siblings. They pulled her in a cart through the meadows and the countryside. Sometimes, Margarete slid along the ground. She always found a way to keep up and have fun.

Margarete went to sewing school and began working so she could save up to buy a sewing machine with her two sisters. Because she couldn't use her right hand, she put the machine back-to-front so the flywheel (the part that spins to move the needle up and down) was on the left side. Then, Margarete and her sisters started a tailoring business. Margarete made long, beautiful skirts out of felt that became very popular.

One day, in December 1879, she was flipping through a magazine when she found a sewing pattern for a stuffed elephant. Margarete went straight to work, sewing bits of felt together and stuffing the elephant with soft lambswool. She planned to make and sell the elephants as pincushions, but as soon as children spotted them, they were in hot demand. The next year, she started her own toy company, and soon she was also designing stuffed monkeys, donkeys, horses, camels, pigs, mice, dogs, and . . . teddy bears!

Margarete's teddy bear was the first-ever stuffed bear with moveable arms and legs. With soft fur, a sturdy torso, and a colorful tag on its ear, Steiff teddy bears were a huge cuddly favorite—and they still are more than a century later.

As Margarete's catalog always said: "For children, only the best is good enough!"

JULY 24, 1847–MAY 9, 1909
GERMANY

"I DISCOVERED THAT I COULD WORK THE MACHINE WITH MY LEFT HAND IF I PUT IT BACK-TO-FRONT BEFORE MY CHAIR. THIS WAS QUITE A DISCOVERY!"
—MARGARETE STEIFF

ILLUSTRATION BY
JENNIFER M. POTTER

SCAN TO HEAR MORE!

MARÍA TERESA KUMAR

VOTING RIGHTS ACTIVIST AND ENTREPRENEUR

María Teresa was nine years old when she and her mom went to a special building in downtown San Francisco, raised their right hands, and recited the Oath of Allegiance to the United States. María Teresa was born in Bogotá, Colombia. Taking the oath meant that she was officially a US citizen—an American. This was a big moment for her.

Growing up in California in the 1980s wasn't easy for María Teresa and her family. Her mom worked long hours to keep food on the table. Her dad was very sick and needed special medical attention.

One day, when María Teresa was 12, she went on a class trip to Washington, DC, and saw lawmakers bustling in and out of the Capitol building. *Do they know what it's like for immigrants in this country?* María Teresa wondered. *What can I do to make them understand? How can I help advance the rights of people like my mom? My aunts? My grandmother?*

María Teresa came up with a plan. She studied government policy, then cofounded a nonprofit organization called Voto Latino that encourages communities to stand up for themselves. It gets young Latinx people excited about voting and making change. María Teresa and her colleagues came up with all sorts of creative ways to get them involved, like offering free rides to the polls and making a bilingual app full of information about voting rights. They even made a hilarious fake soap opera. In the show, a woman dumps her fiancé because he doesn't vote.

So far, Voto Latino has helped more than a million people become agents of change through voting. María Teresa is passionate about making every voice count. As she says, "Let's vote to see the change we need."

BORN JANUARY 31, 1974
COLOMBIA AND UNITED STATES OF AMERICA

ILLUSTRATION BY
ROCEO ARREOLA MENDOZA

"WHAT YOUNG PEOPLE NEED MORE
THAN ANYTHING IS INFORMATION."
—MARÍA TERESA KUMAR

MELANIE PERKINS

ENTREPRENEUR

Every morning, Melanie's alarm went off at 4:30 am. But she didn't mind. She knew her next stop was the skating rink. There, she'd glide across the ice and practice her loops, lutzes, and axels until she landed them with ease. Later, at 14 years old, she channeled her creativity into making scarves, which she took from market to market. Melanie watched as customers wrapped her soft creations around their necks. She realized that she loved the idea of running her own business. It made her feel free.

While in college, Melanie taught computer design as part of her major. She noticed the software the students used was hard to work with. Her entrepreneurial spirit took over.

Melanie created a new program. With it, students and teachers could lay out their own yearbooks—just like expert designers. She approached investors, but they weren't interested. Back to the drawing board she went! Next, she founded a startup called Canva. With Canva, anyone could design what was in their head—eye-catching posters, bold book covers, and lively party invitations.

Still, building her business was a struggle. She had to pitch to more than 100 investors. And finally, she got the funding she needed!

As the company's CEO, Melanie made sure her employees listened to the customers, so they could make the program better and better. Eight years later, Canva was the world's most valuable company with a female founder.

Whether she's spinning on the ice, knitting scarves, or growing her business, Melanie sets crazy big goals and crushes them. And now that she no longer has to wake up at 4:30 am, she has made a rule for herself: Get eight hours of sleep per night for at least 20 days every month.

BORN MAY 13, 1987

AUSTRALIA

ILLUSTRATION BY
JO ZIXUAN

"KNOWING THAT ANY ADVENTURE
WILL BE FILLED WITH REJECTIONS
AND LITTERED WITH OBSTACLES
SOMEHOW MAKES THE ADVENTURE
A LITTLE LESS LONELY."
—MELANIE PERKINS

MIKAILA ULMER

BEE CONSERVATIONIST AND ENTREPRENEUR

After being stung twice in one week, four-year-old Mikaila thought she would be afraid of bees forever.

Her parents suggested she do some research. Maybe then she wouldn't be so scared. Mikaila groaned but took their advice. Soon, she learned that bees are vital to plants because they transfer pollen between them. She also discovered that bees are slowly disappearing as humans and climate change destroy many places where flowers grow.

Buzzing with this information, Mikaila was determined to save the bees.

After her great-granny Helen shared her flaxseed lemonade recipe with the family, Mikaila dreamed up a sweet plan. She would create a new version of the recipe using honey instead of sugar. Then she'd sell the lemonade and donate some of her earnings to bee conservation.

With her mom's help, Mikaila made batches of lemonade—and a sticky mess—in their kitchen. She brought them to sell at a children's business fair, and soon, she was as terrified as she used to be of honeybees! Dressed up in a bee costume, Mikaila wanted to hide, not talk to the customers.

Her concern for bees kept her going, though. And in five years, her business grew from doorstep deliveries to hometown store shelves. Then Mikaila decided to take her pitch to a TV contest for entrepreneurs.

Mikaila prepared for months. On the day of the show, she took a deep breath, faced the panel of five investors, and presented her business in a clear, confident voice. Impressed, one of the judges agreed to invest!

Mikaila and her family have sold more than two million bottles of lemonade. And Mikaila continues to support bees in business and beyond.

BORN SEPTEMBER 28, 2004
UNITED STATES OF AMERICA

"THERE'S NO COOKIE-CUTTER ENTREPRENEUR."
—MIKAILA ULMER

ILLUSTRATION BY
RONIQUE ELLIS

NINA VACA

Nina learned a lot from her mother and father. She learned the importance of working hard, loving her family, supporting her community, and being resilient when things get tough.

Nina's mother and father moved to the United States from Quito, Ecuador, to find new opportunities. They wanted to start their own business, so the whole family could work together.

They tried many different businesses. With each one, Nina was always there after school and on weekends, lending a hand. When her father had a travel agency, 15-year-old Nina sat behind a desk calling airlines and selling tickets. There were times when business was great—and there were times when it wasn't. Some of the companies failed, but no matter what happened, Nina watched as her parents picked themselves up again and again.

The perseverance she learned from them became especially valuable when she was 17. Her father died, and suddenly, Nina needed to step up and help support the family. She and her sister took over their father's travel agency. They sure learned a lot! After a hectic year, Nina knew exactly what she should do next: go to college and get her degree.

Running her father's agency had given Nina a taste for entrepreneurship. After college, at 25 years old, she started a new business, Pinnacle Group, which connects people with job opportunities. It also supports education programs for young people, especially girls and women interested in STEM (science, technology, engineering, and mathematics).

Nina's goal is to show communities around the world how the power of entrepreneurship can change their lives—just like it did hers.

BORN APRIL 1, 1971

ECUADOR AND UNITED STATES OF AMERICA

"THE MOST POWERFUL PEOPLE EMPOWER OTHER PEOPLE."
—NINA VACA

ILLUSTRATION BY MONTSERRAT FREGOSO FONSECA

 # NOURA SAKKIJHA

ENTREPRENEUR

Noura grew up in Jordan. Her parents were entrepreneurs who taught her that if she had a thoughtful idea for a business, she should give it a shot. Because . . . why not?

Her father was a jeweler. Her grandfather was a jeweler. Her cousins were jewelers. They all had that special "why not?" attitude. Noura loved the rich gold and sparkling stones, but she didn't want to join the family business.

Surrounded by numbers and statistics, she studied industrial engineering. Noura learned about all the steps that go into creating a product or gadget. After graduation, she moved to Canada for a new job. Soon, she was getting a business degree. *Maybe it was time for her to start her own company?*

Noura knew the jewelry industry best. But there were a few things about it that bothered her—like the advertising. "Buy this for your wife!" "Give this to your girlfriend!" the ads said. *Why does a women have to wait for someone to give her jewelry?* thought Noura. *She can buy her own necklaces and rings!*

And what about the cost? Most jewelers sold their creations to wholesalers, who sold them into stores. Then the stores sold them to customers. Along the way, the jewelry got more and more expensive. *Wouldn't jewelry be more fun and more accessible if it were affordable?* Noura asked herself.

So she came up with a plan for a company that would skip all the people in the middle and market jewelry straight to women. Together with her partners, Noura launched Mejuri, which sells elegant necklaces, shiny bracelets, and dainty rings that are meant to be mixed, matched, stacked, and worn together or separately. She believes that women should buy the jewelry they want. And they should wear it every day, because . . . why not?

BORN AUGUST 30, 1985
JORDAN AND CANADA

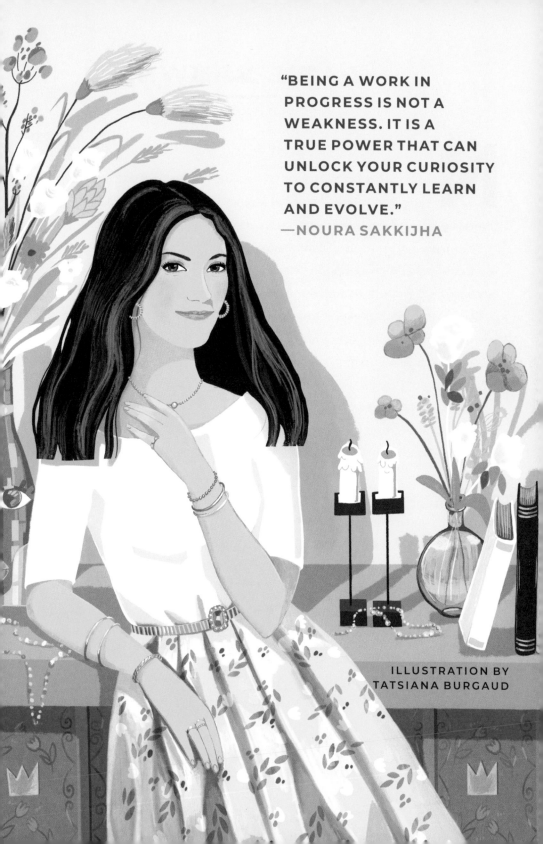

"BEING A WORK IN PROGRESS IS NOT A WEAKNESS. IT IS A TRUE POWER THAT CAN UNLOCK YOUR CURIOSITY TO CONSTANTLY LEARN AND EVOLVE."
—NOURA SAKKIJHA

ILLUSTRATION BY TATSIANA BURGAUD

PAIGE BROWN

ENGINEER AND ENTREPRENEUR

Not long ago, Paige used to splash around and catch frogs in a stream near her house in Maine. The stream and everything in it were like friends who she really cared about.

Then, one day in high school, Paige examined a sample of the stream water for a chemistry project. She was shocked at what she found. Her beloved water was full of poison!

Paige learned that algal blooms had taken over local streams. These were teeny tiny sea plants that bunched together to make bigger ones. The dangerous blooms (which can often be caused by climate change) were toxic, killing the frogs she loved, as well as the fish and other plants. The blooms could hurt people too.

She knew she had to save her stream before it was too late. After studying the problem, Paige turned her basement into a lab, using kitchen equipment as tools. She concocted a special goo made from seaweed gel, then attached it to a device she built with a block of foam and some hair clips. She made mistake after mistake, but seven months later, her invention was complete. It was a water filter that could make her stream clean and safe again. For her amazing work, Paige won a $150,000 college scholarship at a science fair! This inspired her to keep protecting the planet.

Now in her twenties, Paige is cofounder and CEO of Windborne, a company that sends huge balloons—as tall as school buses—into faraway areas (like the middle of a thick forest or high above the Arctic). Devices attached to the balloons gather weather information that scientists can use to help fight climate change. And she owes much of her success to her love of nature.

BORN SEPTEMBER 6, 1998
UNITED STATES OF AMERICA

ILLUSTRATION BY
ALEXANDRA FILIPEK

"I REALIZED THE IMPACT
NATURE HAD ON MY
COMMUNITY AND THE
IMPACT IT HAD ON MY
OWN LIFE."
—PAIGE BROWN

PURVA GUPTA

ENTREPRENEUR

Once there was a girl named Purva who stuttered when she talked. Her family moved from a small town to a glamorous city in northern India when she was just nine years old. Suddenly, Purva felt like she didn't fit in. She earned great grades, but she worried that all the other kids dressed better and spoke better than she did.

Purva's problem wasn't her voice. It was her confidence. A voice inside her told her she wasn't enough. She started to recognize that the mind can be a weakness—or a strength. Over the years, she noticed that when she dressed nicely, her mind felt stronger. When she put on a beautiful outfit or a pair of heels, her stammer went away.

Purva developed a love for clothes, but sometimes, shopping was frustrating. She often bought items just to return them again. And she knew she wasn't the only one. Women buy clothes because they want to look and feel great, she believed, but they often left stores thinking there was something wrong with their bodies or their style.

Purva wanted to help women feel confident. So she started asking shoppers, "What was the last item of clothing you bought, and why?"

The answers came pouring in. What she learned was that shopping is emotional. If retailers asked the right questions and offered more detail about the clothes they sold, people could find more joy—and confidence—in the whole shopping experience. With her new knowledge, Purva cofounded the tech startup Lily AI, which makes shopping more personalized and satisfying.

"What you wear and how you look are intricately related to how you feel," said Purva. And she wants everyone to feel good!

BORN JULY 31, 1988
INDIA AND UNITED STATES OF AMERICA

"WE CAN DO THINGS TO CONDITION OUR OWN MIND TO FEEL MORE CONFIDENT AND REALIZE THE POWER OF OUR OWN MINDSET IN OUR SUCCESS."
—PURVA GUPTA

ILLUSTRATION BY BHAVNA MADAN

RIHANNA

SINGER AND ENTREPRENEUR

Once there was a girl who loved singing, dancing, and celebrating her fabulous brown skin. Rihanna was born on the Caribbean island of Barbados. As a kid, she was always listening to Bob Marley and Madonna and dreaming of being center stage herself.

In high school, Rihanna started an all-girl band with some friends. When a music producer heard her sing, he asked her to live with his family in the United States so he could help launch her career. Rihanna agreed.

Rihanna was just 17 when she released her first single, "Pon de Replay." With reggae dance beats and catchy lyrics, it was a huge success. Two years later, her song "Umbrella" won her a Grammy Award! Rihanna kept on creating new hit songs and dance trends, selling more than 54 million albums and winning eight more Grammy Awards.

But she wanted to explore other forms of art too, so she started a beauty and fashion business.

Her cosmetics line, Fenty Beauty, focuses on inclusivity. Rihanna and her team have made 50 different shades of foundation so everyone can find a shade that matches their skin. And Fenty's models are all different shapes, sizes, and skin colors.

Rihanna also designed a clothing line and became the first Black woman in charge of a major luxury fashion house. She is passionate about following her dreams wherever they lead her.

That's why she has a tattoo written backwards on her shoulder. So she can always read it in the mirror and feel the power of its message: "Never a failure. Always a lesson."

BORN FEBRUARY 20, 1988
BARBADOS AND UNITED STATES OF AMERICA

ILLUSTRATION BY
JESTENIA
SOUTHERLAND

"MAKEUP IS THERE
FOR YOU TO HAVE FUN
WITH. . . . FEEL FREE
TO TAKE CHANCES AND
TAKE RISKS AND DARE
TO DO SOMETHING NEW
OR DIFFERENT."
—RIHANNA

SARAH FRIAR

BUSINESS EXECUTIVE

Once upon a time, 10-year-old Sarah heard a thunderous *boom!* The windows in her house shattered. A nearby bomb had just exploded. Sadly, at the time, it was a common occurrence in Northern Ireland where Sarah lived.

Although terrified, she was also comforted by all the neighbors who rushed over with plywood to help her family board up their windows. These were the same folks from her farming village who often knocked on her family's door at night. Sometimes they needed her mother, who was a nurse, and sometimes they needed her father, who was a manager at the local mill. They might ask them for medical care, money, or a job. She loved having a community where everyone pitched in, in times of need.

So when Sarah got older and moved to Ghana, Africa, to work as an engineer in a gold mine, she was surprised at how unwelcome she felt. It was difficult being the only woman in her office, where she was told to make the men tea rather than do her real job. She soon left and moved to the United States to work in business.

Sarah loved being the CFO (chief financial officer) of a huge company, but then, Nextdoor—an online platform that connects people with their real-life neighbors—asked her to be their CEO. She couldn't refuse! Bringing back childhood memories, she took charge of a growing company that helps neighbors look out for one another, ask about jobs, and discuss local schools. Members form book clubs, plan block parties, and make good friends. Rather than connecting neighbors in a small village, she is connecting millions of neighbors in 11 countries around the world.

BORN DECEMBER 24, 1972
NORTHERN IRELAND AND UNITED STATES OF AMERICA

ILLUSTRATION BY
DOROTA JANICKA

SAN FRANCISCO

"AS A LEADER, THE
PHRASE I USE ALL THE
TIME IS 'PEOPLE FIRST.'
GET YOUR PEOPLE RIGHT,
AND EVERYTHING ELSE
JUST WORKS."
—SARAH FRIAR

SOLVEIGA PAKŠTAITĖ

INVENTOR AND ENTREPRENEUR

Solveiga was a curious Lithuanian girl growing up in the United Kingdom. She had light brown hair, bright red glasses, and a mind that was always asking questions—questions like: *Why do some people live in poverty and others have more than enough? How can we take care of our planet?* And, *What can we do to make sure everyone feels included?*

In college, Solveiga studied inclusive design, which is about coming up with ideas and inventions that help people of all abilities thrive. She was determined to create a tool that could assist everyone in some way. She talked to lots of people living with vision impairments.

How do you know when your food is expired? she asked them.

Many people couldn't see the tiny dates printed on packaged foods. When Solveiga dug deeper, she learned that even when they *could* see those printed dates, they're not always accurate. People end up throwing away perfectly good food. In fact, 70% of the food thrown away in the UK is safe to eat. What a waste!

Solveiga designed a solution to this global problem. She created a company consisting of engineers and an all-women team of scientists and, together, they made a label that measures food's freshness. When the food is good, the label feels smooth. When the food expires, the label turns bumpy. The brilliant invention is already saving tons of meat, milk, and juice from being wasted, and she hopes it will be on lots of food packages soon.

Solveiga's company is called Mimica, and its mission is to always be curious and create change that helps people and the planet.

BORN MAY 21, 1992

LITHUANIA, NORWAY, AND UNITED KINGDOM

ILLUSTRATION BY
THAIZ ZAFALON

"IT'S CRAZY TO THINK
THAT PEOPLE ARE
GOING HUNGRY YET SO
MUCH GOOD FOOD IS
GOING TO WASTE."
—SOLVEIGA PAKŠTAITĖ

STACY BROWN-PHILPOT

BUSINESS EXECUTIVE

When Stacy and her brother were little, they set up their own newspaper delivery service in Detroit, Michigan. Together, they convinced some neighbors to buy the paper from them instead of getting it at the store. Her brother always delivered the papers on time. And, since they made money by charging a delivery fee, 11-year-old Stacy went out to collect payments whether the sun was shining or the temperatures were below freezing. Her mom worked tirelessly to take care of the family, and Stacy followed her example.

After college, Stacy took a job at a huge tech company. She enjoyed it, but when she glanced around, she saw few people who looked like her. So she started a program to recruit more employees from historically Black colleges and universities. She wanted to make it easier for more young Black women and men to pursue careers in high-paying fields.

Stacy then joined a startup called TaskRabbit. The company specializes in matching workers to quick jobs. The workers, or "taskers," do things like run errands for their clients or help them around the house.

Three years later, in 2016, Stacy became the CEO—one of the only Black female CEOs in the tech industry. She made sure that all employees, including herself, worked as taskers. Stacy once spent the day with someone who had no idea the person scrubbing their oven was the company's CEO!

With Stacy in charge, TaskRabbit expanded to thousands of cities.

Ready for another adventure, she later teamed up with two other investors to create a fund to support Black, Latinx, and Native American founders.

BORN OCTOBER 27, 1975
UNITED STATES OF AMERICA

ILLUSTRATION BY
RAFAELA RIJO-NÚÑEZ

"THERE ARE SO MANY DIFFERENT WAYS
THAT EACH OF US AS INDIVIDUALS CAN
IMPACT THE COMMUNITIES AROUND US."
—STACY BROWN-PHILPOT

URSULA BURNS

BUSINESS EXECUTIVE

Once upon a time, Ursula dreamed of a career she didn't see. She wanted to be an engineer, but there weren't any engineers in her life to look to for inspiration or go to for advice. Throughout high school, her teachers only ever talked about girls becoming nurses, teachers, or nuns.

When it came time for college, Ursula wasn't sure what to do. Should she go to school for nursing or teaching? Should she enter a convent? Or should she go after her goal?

Her mother loved to say, "Where you are is not who you are."

It was with those words echoing in her heart that Ursula decided to apply to engineering school. She was excited! But she was also terrified at the thought of getting accepted. The school was so different from everything and everyone she knew. And when she got in, her fear only grew.

Ursula was a rare Black girl on a campus of mostly white students. She had to take extra courses to catch up to the material they studied. As she struggled to balance her schoolwork with her completely new environment, Ursula wondered, *Do I have what it takes to become an engineer?*

Once again, her mother's words rang in her ear, urging her to look beyond what she could see. In Ursula's last year of college, she took an internship at a company even farther away from home. Xerox was a Fortune 500 company (one of the 500 most profitable corporations in the entire United States). She did such a great job there, they hired her after graduation. For the next 37 years, she worked her way up until she became the first Black woman CEO of a Fortune 500 company. She made sure everyone could see her and became an inspiration to underrepresented kids everywhere.

BORN SEPTEMBER 20, 1958
UNITED STATES OF AMERICA

"LEAVE BEHIND MORE THAN YOU TAKE AWAY."
—URSULA BURNS

ILLUSTRATION BY KELSEE THOMAS

WHITNEY WOLFE HERD

ANTI-BULLYING ACTIVIST AND ENTREPRENEUR

Once upon a time, Whitney was a happy girl in Utah who loved to ski, camp, and obsess over Walt Disney. She was fascinated that someone could create such a magical world.

But after college, her happiness turned sour. In her early twenties, she cofounded a popular dating app. It was thrilling to be part of a successful startup. But when she broke up with her boyfriend, who worked with her, it was like a wicked storm blew into her life. Suddenly, her ex-boyfriend and coworkers turned against her, and she was forced to quit her job. Then strangers on social media got wind of her troubles and began to bully her online. The whole world seemed cruel.

Sometimes, she wanted to just curl up and hide. She hated that some people could be so mean. *How can I create a place filled with kindness and understanding?* Whitney wondered. She imagined her own magical world where bullies would be locked out! *Could she turn this idea into an app?*

She drew up a plan and shared it with a fellow entrepreneur, who invested in her vision for Bumble, a friendship and dating app where negative comments are not permitted. To make sure women aren't harassed, men are not allowed to ask them out—women get to make the first move. Now, Whitney runs her dream business out of a yellow building called The Hive, with a large "Bee Kind" sign and furniture shaped like honeycombs.

Whitney has started a fund to invest in other female founders, especially women of color. She's also the youngest woman to take a company public, allowing others to buy shares (or small portions) of her company and join in the magical world she built.

BORN JULY 1, 1989

UNITED STATES OF AMERICA

"I HATED THE WAY I WAS TREATED ONLINE. IT SCARED ME, AND INSTEAD OF LETTING THAT BURY ME, I DECIDED TO GO OUT AND BUILD A SOLUTION."
—WHITNEY WOLFE HERD

ILLUSTRATION BY ANNA DIXON

WRITE YOUR STORY

DRAW YOUR PORTRAIT

BUSINESS WORDS

There are lots of words used in the business world that may not be familiar to you. Learn these and you'll be ready to launch your entrepreneurial journey!

BUSINESS BASICS

An **entrepreneur** is someone who creates, builds, or runs a business. Entrepreneurs often dream up solutions to problems that exist in the world and then build products or services to fix them. They start new companies (as founders) or grow young companies and work hard to make them succeed. Being an entrepreneur is exciting! But it can also be stressful, because starting a new business is risky and growing a business is challenging. Not all businesses succeed.

A person who has started more than one business is known as a **serial entrepreneur**. Some of the serial entrepreneurs in this book are Jennifer Doudna (page 14) and Mar Hershenson (page 26).

A new business is a **startup**, and you will read about many of them in this book, including the Cheeky Panda (page 16) and Lily AI (page 42).

Most businesses sell a **product** (a thing a person can buy, like a coat, teddy bear, or a video game) or a **service** (an action a person performs, like shoveling snow, weeding a garden, or hosting a hilarious YouTube channel). In order for a business to thrive, it needs **customers**, or people who buy what the company is offering.

For-profit companies offer products or services that are valuable to customers and generate revenue. **Nonprofit organizations** are different. They usually have a social mission, and they generally collect money through **fundraising** efforts. Employees ask people and other companies for **donations** (gifts of money or items that they need). They also apply for **grants**, which are financial contributions from institutions and from the government. The American Heart Association and Voto Latino (page 30) are examples of nonprofit organizations. Nike and Canva (page 32) are examples of for-profit companies.

WHAT IS A C-SUITE?

The executives who lead a company make up the **C-suite**. The C in C-suite stands for "chief." At the head of the company is the **CEO (chief executive officer)**. CEOs are in charge of creating a company's strategy and vision, and steering a company and its employees toward its goals. The **CFO (chief financial officer)** and the **CTO (chief technology officer)** are some of the other executives who are often part of the C-suite.

The CEO reports to the **board of directors**, who oversees the CEO and the strategy, financial responsibility, and progress of a company. A board of directors can be made up of people who've invested their money in the company, independent members who bring expert skills in different fields, and some of the key employees (such as the CEO). The best boards have all sorts of skills and backgrounds so they make decisions incorporating a variety of ideas.

PRIVATE OR PUBLIC?

Privately owned companies are owned by the founders, investors, or managers of the business. When a private company needs funds to grow, it might ask a bank for a loan or offer **shares**, or portions of the company, to investors who invest in the company's future. **Venture capitalists** are one type of investor who invests in private companies.

A **public company** is different. Part or all of the company is owned by the public, also in the form of shares. **Shareholders** own pieces of the company and can share in the company's profits. They get to vote on who the board of directors will be. The more shares a person owns, the more influence they have.

WHAT DOES IT MEAN TO "TAKE A COMPANY PUBLIC"?

Shares of public companies are traded on the stock market, where investors buy and sell stocks, or shares, of companies. To become a public company, a business has an IPO, an initial public offering. During an IPO, companies generally raise lots of money by selling shares. Many CEOs wait until their company is valued at $1 billion or more before they take it public. A company valued at $1 billion is known as a unicorn. In 2021, at 31, Whitney Wolfe Herd (page 54) became the youngest woman founder to take her company public.

BUILD YOUR OWN BUSINESS

Grab a pen and some paper and get ready to give your entrepreneurial brain a workout. These activities were designed by business leader Jocelyn Mangan, of Him For Her, to help you start your own business.

STEP 1: BRAINSTORM, BRAINSTORM, BRAINSTORM

To come up with a strong business idea, start with the things that interest you. Answer these questions—in words or pictures.

- What do you like to do most?
- When you get up in the morning, what are you most excited to do?
- What are your hobbies and interests?

My Interests
Ballet
Dogs
Playing video games

STEP 2: WHAT CAN YOU MAKE OR DO?

Think about how you can translate your interests into a business. Answer the questions below to help brainstorm products or services you could provide.

- What can you create or do to make your hobby or interest better, more fun, or easier to do?
- What can you create or do to share your hobby or interest with others?
- How can you use your interests to help others?

What I Can Make or Do
- Homemade scrunchies for dancers
- Dog-walking service
- Code my own video game

STEP 3: DEFINE YOUR BUSINESS

Choose the item you want to make or the service you want to offer. Then answer the questions below.

- What did you choose? What is its purpose?
- Who is going to buy your product or hire you?
- What might make someone want to buy this product or service?

STEP 4: NAME YOUR COMPANY

Brainstorm words that describe the business you are building.
Have fun with it!

- Write down potential company names. As you pick your favorite, make sure it sounds good when you say it out loud.
- If your company name is made up of more than one word, try out an acronym for the name. An acronym is formed from the first letter of each word in the name. (For example, ABC is the acronym for the American Broadcasting Company.)

STEP 5: CREATE YOUR COMPANY LOGO

Using art supplies or your computer, design a logo. A logo is
a symbol or picture that represents your company.

- Your logo might spell out the name of your business or show its acronym.
- Add a picture or some doodles that help explain what your company offers. You can also draw or color in the letters in a way that shows something about your business.

STEP 6: BUILD A PROTOTYPE

If you plan to make and sell something, now's the time to make a prototype. A prototype is a model or sample of your product.

- With a grown-up's help, buy or collect any items or equipment you may need.
- Make a version of your product. Whether you are baking cupcakes or building a video game, you may want to try out a few versions to see what looks or works best.

STEP 7: TEST IT OUT

Once your prototype is ready, make sure it works. This is called beta testing. A beta is a nearly finished version of your product.

- Have some friends or family members test your beta. Ask lots of questions. How do your scrunchies work? Does your dog-walking service operate during the hours when people need it most?

- If your company is about selling a service, test it out. Ask a family friend or neighbor to test out your dog-walking or gardening service. Take notes about what works best and what needs improvement.

- Keep making prototypes until you've got the best version of your product or service.

> **IT'S OKAY TO FAIL**
>
> **The first versions of products and services often fail. Remember: That's okay! Testing out your product or service helps you make it better.**

STEP 8: MATH TIME!

For your business to be successful, you need to be able to earn more money than you spend. Let's make a budget.

- Make a list of all of the materials or equipment you need to get your business started. Then write down how much each of these things costs. Add them up. Those costs are your expenses.

- Look at your expenses. Divide your total costs by the number of products you can make with those materials.

Budget

Revenue	Amount	Expenses	Costs
		1 yard fabric	$13
		1.5 yards elastic	$2
		Scissors	$0
		Sewing kit	$0
Total Revenue	$	Total Expenses	$15

Number of scrunchies I can make with $15 worth of materials: 20

Cost per scrunchie:
$15 ÷ 20= $0.75

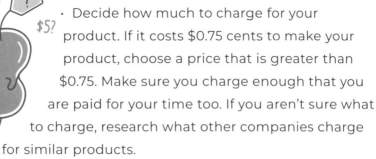

- Decide how much to charge for your product. If it costs $0.75 cents to make your product, choose a price that is greater than $0.75. Make sure you charge enough that you are paid for your time too. If you aren't sure what to charge, research what other companies charge for similar products.

- On the same sheet as your expenses, add your revenue. This is the amount of money you earn from your company's sales.

- Subtract your total expenses from your total revenue. That's how you can find out how much profit your company should make.

Budget

Revenue	Amount	Expenses	Costs
1 scrunchie	$5	1 yard fabric	$13
3 scrunchies	$15	1.5 yards elastic	$2
2 scrunchies	$10	Scissors	$0
1 scrunchie	$5	Sewing kit	$0
Total Revenue	$35	Total Expenses	$15

Profit and Loss Statement

Total Revenue	$35
Total Expenses	$15
Profit (or loss, if this is a negative number)	$20

Mikaila Ulmer (page 34) charges $29.99 for 10 bottles of her special lemonade. That's $2.99 per bottle.

STEP 9: FUND YOUR COMPANY

It takes money to start a company. How will you get the money you need? Do you have savings? Maybe you can approach investors (like some grown-ups you trust) to see if they are interested in investing in your business.

- Write down your plan to fund your company. If you decide to approach investors, you'll need to tell them how you plan to earn enough money to pay them back.
- Before you approach investors, you will need an exciting pitch. Write a short description of your company. In it, explain why your company is different from others and why people will want to buy your product or service. Practice your pitch out loud. Say it in front of a mirror until you are feeling confident.

STEP 10: SPREAD THE WORD

To be a success, a company needs customers. How will you find them? How will you let them know about what your company has to offer?

- Write a slogan—a short, fun description of your product or service. A good slogan catches people's attention. Try setting your slogan to music to make a catchy jingle. Then create a video using your jingle!
- Design an advertisement for your product—like the ones you see online or on TV.

Magi Richani's (page 24) company makes dairy-free cheese. On the Nobell Foods website, you might see the slogan. "Say cheese. Think plants."

STEP 11: BUILD YOUR TEAM

Imagine a venture capitalist has just made a big investment in your company. Who will you hire to help your business grow?

- Do you need more crafters or dog walkers? Maybe you'd like to hire someone who writes great social media posts to help you attract new customers? Or maybe you'd like to hire an artist to jazz up your advertisements? Brainstorm a list of jobs. Then draw your dream team.
- What skills will you be looking for? Now, write job descriptions for each of the employees you would like to hire.

STEP 12: CHOOSE A MENTOR

When you are starting out in business, there is so much to learn. One way to explore your ideas and pick up new skills is to enlist the help of a mentor.

- Think of a grown-up who you would like to learn from. What would you like to learn from them? What questions would you ask?
- Write a letter introducing yourself to a potential mentor. Describe your business and why you think they could offer you advice or encouragement as you become an entrepreneur.

ABOUT HIM FOR HER

Founded in 2018, Him For Her is a nonprofit company that aims to change boards of directors to include the world's most talented women. As CEO, Jocelyn Mangan is building the boardrooms of the future. She partners with the world's top leaders and investors to uncover more board opportunities for more women. Since its founding in 2018, Him For Her has built a large talent network of board-ready women, helping thousands find more opportunities to take a board seat and change the world.

www.himforher.org

SUPER SLIME SHOPPE

We asked kids in the KiwiCo community what kinds of businesses they've started. Here's what they've done:

- Julia teaches the little kids in her neighborhood how to play soccer.
- Fiona learned how to crochet and started to make cup cozies that she and her sister sell online.
- Ella started to make slime—some with glitter, some that glow, and some with scents—to sell to her classmates at school.

HERE'S ELLA'S SUPER SLIME RECIPE:

Super Slime Recipe

You'll need...

2 small disposable cups
Measuring Spoons
Pipette
Water
Borax
Glue

Directions

1. Make a borax mixture. Fill a small cup with 4–6 Tbsp of water. Add 1 tsp of borax. Mix for at least 30 seconds to break up lumps.

2. Make a glue mixture. Add 2 Tbsp of water to a separate small cup. Add 1 Tbsp of glue. Then, mix until smooth.

3. Make the slime. Use a pipette to squirt the borax mixture into the glue mixture and mix. Add more borax (4–8 squirts) until the glue clumps together. Scrape the slime out of the cup and knead it until the slime comes together. Optional: Add glitter, glow powder, or confetti.

4. Sell it! Package up your slime, and you're ready to start selling—or head to KiwiCo for kits to make slime or soap or hats and get a jump-start on making products for your own business!

ABOUT KIWICO

KiwiCo designs and delivers fun and enriching hands-on activities for kids. From chemistry experiments and art projects to mechanical games and pretend play, KiwiCo inspires the next generation of innovators and makers. KiwiCo was founded by Sandra Oh Lin.

LISTEN TO MORE EMPOWERING STORIES ON THE REBEL GIRLS APP!

Download the app to listen to beloved Rebel Girls stories, as well as brand-new tales of extraordinary women. Filled with the adventures and accomplishments of women from around the world and throughout history, the Rebel Girls app is designed to entertain, inspire, and build confidence in listeners everywhere.

THE ILLUSTRATORS

Twenty-five extraordinary female and nonbinary artists from all over the world illustrated the portraits in this book.

ALEXANDRA FILIPEK, USA, 41

ANDRESSA MEISSNER, BRAZIL, 9

ANNA DIXON, USA, 55

BHAVNA MADAN, INDIA, 43

CARIBAY MB, ARGENTINA, 25

CRISTINA SPANÒ, ITALY, 23

DOROTA JANICKA, POLAND, 47

FABIOLA F. ALDRETE SOLORIO, MEXICO, 19

IRENE RINALDI, ITALY, 15

JENNIFER M POTTER, USA, 29

JESTENIA SOUTHERLAND, USA, 45

JO ZIXUAN, CHINA, 33

KATHRIN HONESTA, INDONESIA, 7

KELSEE THOMAS, USA, 53

LILY NIE, AUSTRALIA, 17

MAJU BENGEL, BRAZIL, 27

MONTSERRAT FREGOSO FONSECA, MEXICO, 37

NAKI NARH, UK, 11

PAU ZAMRO, MEXICO, 21

RAFAELA RIJO-NÚÑEZ, GERMANY, 51

ROCEO ARREOLA MENDOZA, MEXICO, 31

RONIQUE ELLIS, JAMAICA, 35

TATSIANA BURGAUD, FRANCE, 39

THAIZ ZAFALON, BRAZIL, 49

XUAN LOC XUAN, VIETNAM, 13

ABOUT REBEL GIRLS

REBEL GIRLS is a global, multi-platform empowerment brand dedicated to helping raise the most inspired and confident global generation of girls through content, experiences, products, and community. Originating from an international best-selling children's book, Rebel Girls amplifies stories of real-life women throughout history, geography, and field of excellence. With a growing community of nearly 20 million self-identified Rebel Girls spanning more than 100 countries, the brand engages with Generation Alpha through its book series, award-winning podcast, events, and merchandise. With the 2021 launch of the Rebel Girls app, the company has created a flagship destination for girls to explore a wondrous world filled with inspiring true stories of extraordinary women.

Join the Rebel Girls' community:

- Facebook: facebook.com/rebelgirls
- Instagram: @rebelgirls
- Twitter: @rebelgirlsbook
- Web: rebelgirls.com
- App: rebelgirls.com/app

If you liked this book, please take a moment to review it wherever you prefer!

READ MORE!